THE CHECKLIST CHALLENGE GUIDE TO SUMMER

BY BLAKE A. HOENA

Raintree is an imprint of Capstone Global Library Limited, a company incorporated in England and Wales having its registered office at 264 Banbury Road, Oxford, OX2 7DY – Registered company number: 6695582

www.raintree.co.uk
myorders@raintree.co.uk

Text © Capstone Global Library Limited 2024
Paperback edition published in 2025

The moral rights of the proprietor have been asserted. All rights reserved. No part of this publication may be reproduced in any form or by any means (including photocopying or storing it in any medium by electronic means and whether or not transiently or incidentally to some other use of this publication) without the written permission of the copyright owner, except in accordance with the provisions of the Copyright, Designs and Patents Act 1988 or under the terms of a licence issued by the Copyright Licensing Agency, 5th Floor, Shackleton House, 4 Battle Bridge Lane, London, SE1 2HX (www.cla.co.uk). Applications for the copyright owner's written permission should be addressed to the publisher.

Editorial Credits
Editor: Donald Lemke; Designer: Kay Fraser; Media Researchers: Jo Miller and Svetlana Zhurkin; Production Specialist: Katy LaVigne

ISBN 978 1 3982 5211 0 (hardback)
ISBN 978 1 3982 5216 5 (paperback)

British Library Cataloguing in Publication Data
A full catalogue record for this book is available from the British Library.

Image credits
Getty Images: anton5146, 20, Caiaimage/Martin Barraud, 12, Cyndi Monaghan, 26, Dieter Meyrl, 11, Ed Bock, 14, FatCamera, 24, Joe McBride, 21, kali9, cover (bottom right), Nadezhda1906, 6, PeopleImages, 13, SW Productions, 29 (bottom), Tetra Images/Erik Isakson, cover (bottom left), Thinkstock, 18, Trevor Williams, 10, Zabavna, 15; Shutterstock: anatoliy_gleb, 9, Carolyn Franks, 27, Donna Lupgens, 29 (middle), interstid, 8, Jess Kraft, 29 (top), LightField Studios, 19, Matthieu Cattin, 17, Odua Images, 16, oneinchpunch, 25, Pixel-Shot, 22, Prostock-studio, 23, Rohappy, cover (left), VGstockstudio, 5, VH-studio, 7, ViDI Studio, 4

Every effort has been made to contact copyright holders of material reproduced in this book. Any omissions will be rectified in subsequent printings if notice is given to the publisher.

All the internet addresses (URLs) given in this book were valid at the time of going to press. However, due to the dynamic nature of the internet, some addresses may have changed, or sites may have changed or ceased to exist since publication. While the author and publisher regret any inconvenience this may cause readers, no responsibility for any such changes can be accepted by either the author or the publisher.

CONTENTS

SCHOOL'S OUT 4
THE GREAT OUTDOORS 6
GET CREATIVE 12
GO ON AN ADVENTURE 18
GET YOUR PLAY ON 22
WANT TO TRY MORE? 28
GLOSSARY 30
FIND OUT MORE 31
INDEX 32
ABOUT THE AUTHOR 32

Words in **bold** appear in the glossary.

☑ SCHOOL'S OUT

Summer's here! You don't have to worry about homework, so have some fun. But how will you tackle all the exciting things you imagine doing? Start by creating a checklist!

Write down all the thrills you want to experience during the summer holidays. Then, as you get to each one, tick them off your list. You'll have a record of all the fun you had!

☑ THE GREAT OUTDOORS

CREATE A PERSONAL FIELD GUIDE

Summer is all about getting out and enjoying nature. Go for walk along the beach, through the field or around a park. Along the way, you'll see all sorts of beautiful wildlife.

Create a personal field guide of birds, fish, insects and other animals you see. You can take pictures or, if you're **artistic**, draw everything you discover. You can also write down the places you visit and the sights you see. Nothing is off-limits!

CAMP OUT!

To **immerse** yourself in nature, go camping! Spend a few nights in the great outdoors. You can cook over a campfire and go on nature walks.

The UK's national parks are great places to camp. They provide a chance to add to your field guide. Also, while away from city or town lights, you'll be able to do some great **stargazing**.

ROCK CLIMBING

If you're **adventurous,** try an activity like rock climbing. Not only will it be a challenge, but it'll be a great way to impress your friends.

Rock climbing will allow you to reach new heights. You can see great views from the top of a cliff. Just make sure you go with an experienced rock climber. Find someone who has all the gear you'll need for a safe adventure.

☑ GET CREATIVE

BUILD A FAB FORT!

With the freedom of summer, you'll have time to take up a new hobby or activity. You'll have a chance to get creative.

How you **express** your creativity is all up to you. It could be building a den or fort in your garden. You can decorate your new hangout place however you like. Then you and your friends will have a cool place to chill.

GROW A POLLINATOR GARDEN

Be creative by designing a **pollinator** garden. Plant flowers that attract helpful pollinators, such as bees and butterflies. They will look pretty and will give the bees and butterflies a food source. All the pollinators you see can be added to the field guide you've already made!

FOUND ART PROJECT

A found art project gives you a chance to both help nature and get creative.

With friends and family, make it your **mission** to pick up **litter** in your area or at a local park. From plastic bottles to cans, you could find items to create something artistic.

☑ GO ON AN ADVENTURE

PLAN A BIKE RIDE

Summer is the time for adventures, both near and far. You could go on a bike ride with your friends. Decide on a **destination**. It could be a friend's house, a favourite ice-cream shop or a park.

Once you have decided where to go, use a smartphone to plan your route. Before you pedal away, make sure you take some snacks for energy and water to stay **hydrated**.

GO TO AN AMUSEMENT PARK

To get some true thrills, visit a theme park. If you go with friends, challenge each other to see who rides the scariest rollercoaster.

What an adventure! Add going to a theme park to your checklist.

☑ GET YOUR PLAY ON

GAME NIGHT

Do you and your friends have a favourite video game? Then what could be a better way to hang out than by having a game night. Add this to your checklist. And don't forget to get some of your favourite snacks!

DISC GOLF

Are you into sport? You could always meet your friends at the park and have a fun game of baksetball or tennis. Or you could even play a sport you might not have tried before, such as disc golf. All it takes is a couple of discs. You'll be hanging out with friends and enjoying time outside.

GARDEN MOVIE NIGHT

You and your friends share some favourite films. Plan a movie night while enjoying the summer weather. You can use the side of a house or hang up a sheet for the screen. Make sure you have plenty of popcorn! Add sports and movie night to your summer checklist.

WANT TO TRY MORE?

You've got all the important checklist items for a solid summer! Now it's time to add some extra activities and experiences to your must-do list. Check out (and then check off) a few of these ideas. Then think of other items to add to the list!

- ☑ Go fishing.
- ☑ Watch the birds.
- ☑ Stargaze and find constellations.
- ☑ Have a picnic with friends.
- ☑ Make a film with your smartphone.
- ☑ Build a sandcastle.
- ☑ Draw your own comic book.
- ☑ Go canoeing or surfing.
- ☑ Visit a national park.
- ☑ Watch fireworks.

GLOSSARY

adventurous open to adventure or dealing with the new and unknown

artistic being skilled at painting, making things or performing in the arts

destination place that a person or vehicle is travelling to

express show what you feel or think by saying, doing or writing something

hydrated having enough water

immerse completely involve yourself in something

litter rubbish scattered around carelessly

mission special job or task

pollinator something, often an insect, that carries pollen from one flower to another

stargaze look at the stars

FIND OUT MORE

BOOKS

Be Confident Be You, Becky Goddard-Hill (Collins, 2023)

Little Country Cottage: A Summer Treasury of Recipes, Crafts and Wisdom, Angela Ferraro-Fanning (Ivy Kids Eco, 2022)

You Are a Champion: How to Be the Best You Can Be, Marcus Rashford (MacMillan, 2021)

WEBSITES

www.bbc.co.uk/cbbc/quizzes/sporty-summer-holiday-activity-finder
Not sure what to do over the summer holidays? This CBBC quiz can help you.

www.sitters.co.uk/blog/22-great-family-days-out-this-summer.aspx
Plan some great days out with the Sitters website.

INDEX

basketball 24

camping, 9

cycling 18–19

disc golf 24

field guide 7, 9, 15

forts 13

found art 16

gardening 15

homework 4

movie night 27

national parks 9

nature 6, 9, 15, 16

pollinator garden 15

rock climbing 10–11

stargazing 9

tennis 24

theme parks 21

video games 22

ABOUT THE AUTHOR

Blake Hoena grew up in central Wisconsin, USA, where he wrote stories about robots conquering the Moon and trolls lumbering around the woods behind his parents' house. He now lives in the state of Minnesota and enjoys writing about fun things like history, space aliens and superheroes. Blake has written more than 50 chapter books and dozens of graphic novels for children.